The Human Touch Performance Appraisal

Charles M. Cadwell

American Media Publishing
4900 University Avenue
West Des Moines, Iowa 50266-6769
800-262-2557

The Human Touch Performance Appraisal

Charles M. Cadwell
Copyright © 1994 by American Media Incorporated

This publication is designed to provide accurate and authoritative information in regard to the subject matter covered. It is sold with the understanding that neither the author nor the publisher is engaged in rendering legal, accounting, or other professional service. If legal advice or other expert assistance is required, the services of a competent professional should be sought.

Credits:

American Media Publishing:	Arthur Bauer
	Todd McDonald
	Leigh Lewis
Editor in Chief:	Karen Massetti Miller
Editor:	Dave Kirchner
Designer:	Gayle O'Brien
Cover Design:	Maura Rombalski

Published by American Media Inc.
4900 University Avenue
West Des Moines, IA 50266-6769

Library of Congress Catalog Card Number 97-03105
Cadwell, Charles M.
The Human Touch Performance Appraisal

Printed in the United States of America
1998
ISBN 1-884926-23-1

About the Author

Charles M. Cadwell is the president of Training Systems +, a Kansas company that specializes in training system design and development. He has nearly 20 years of experience in the training field.

Prior to starting Training Systems + in 1986, Mr. Cadwell held positions as Director of Field Training for Pizza Hut, Inc. and Director of Training for Popingo Video. His clients have included such Fortune 500 companies as PepsiCo Food Service International, Pizza Hut, Inc., Frito-Lay, Rent-A-Center, and Burger King International. He also has worked with a number of small-to medium-size retail and manufacturing businesses.

Mr. Cadwell's first book, *New Employee Orientation*, was published in 1988. Since then, he has written three audiocassette programs on the subjects of recruiting and selection, orientation and training, and leadership skills. He is also coauthor of *50 Activities for Coaching and Mentoring*, which was published in 1993.

Mr. Cadwell is past president of the Sunflower Chapter of the American Society for Training and Development.

Acknowledgments

The author wishes to thank Mark Neeley, National Training Manager for Rent-A-Center, and Arthur Bauer and Todd McDonald at American Media Incorporated for their valuable contributions to this book.

Introduction

The Human Touch Performance Appraisal focuses on the process of conducting performance appraisals, not the paperwork or the "form." Applying the human touch helps managers get the most from their employees; it's a way to show employees that they sincerely care enough to listen to their goals, wants, needs, and expectations. Managers who implement the human touch build on their employees' strengths and help them reach their true potential.

Your organization may have a well-designed form that takes into account every possible aspect of the employee's performance. Or you may use a simple one-page fill-in-the-blanks form. But in the end, it's not the form that matters. It's the process that counts.

The interaction between manager and employee is what makes or breaks the success of any performance appraisal.

Many managers dread the thought of conducting performance appraisals. Yet, when they're done correctly, performance appraisals give you an important opportunity to help yourself, as well as your employees and your organization.

This book will help you prepare for successful performance appraisals, and it will help you prepare your employees too. You'll find lots of helpful hints to make the process run more smoothly. And as you read, you'll have opportunities to evaluate yourself, and develop any needed plans for improvement.

In the end, everything depends on the effort you make to apply this material to the performance appraisals you conduct. When you adopt the caring approach of the human touch performance-appraisal process, appraisal time can be one both you and your employees actually look forward to!

Book Objectives

Objectives help us define the direction we need to take to reach a goal. They're like a road map to guide us on our journey. Without objectives, it's easy to wind up someplace we didn't really want to go.

This book has just one purpose—to help you develop and apply the human touch to your performance appraisals.

After reading this book and completing its exercises, you should be able to:

◆ Apply the human touch to your performance appraisals.

◆ Describe the purposes and benefits of a performance appraisal.

◆ Prepare to conduct an appraisal discussion.

◆ Conduct an effective appraisal discussion.

◆ Follow up on your performance appraisals.

◆ Maintain an effective performance-appraisal system.

You may have some additional goals of your own. If so, write them here:

_____

_____

_____

_____

_____

Chapter *One*

Getting Started

Chapter Objectives

▶ List the three steps of the human touch performance-appraisal process.

▶ Describe the purposes and benefits of performance appraisals.

▶ Explain the link between salary administration and performance appraisals.

The *human touch* is the performance-appraisal process that puts people first.

The *human touch* is the performance-appraisal process that puts people first. When managers apply the human touch, they get the most from their employees because they show that they care enough to listen to them. These managers go out of their way to demonstrate that they care about their employees' hopes, dreams, and concerns. The human touch approach encourages employees to build on their strengths and realize their true potential.

Remember that an important reason employees work is to realize their dreams, visions, and goals. As a manager, you can help them do just that by taking the time to discuss those aspirations with them.

To realize the many benefits of the human touch, you need merely make a commitment to the kind of performance-appraisal process that gets results. Managers who practice the techniques and procedures described in this book should see the results in the improved performance of their employees.

The Human Touch Perfromance Appraisal Process

Implementing the human touch is a three-step process of:

◆ Preparing for the meeting

◆ Conducting the appraisal meeting

◆ Following up

The diagram below shows the human touch performance-appraisal process that is described in this book.

1. Preparing for the Meeting

2. Conducting the Appraisal Meeting

3. Following Up

Preparing for the Meeting

Preparation is key to achieving the results you want from your performance appraisal. In most cases, the time you invest preparing for an appraisal meeting will exceed the time you spend in the meeting itself. The preparation steps outlined in this book will start you on the right track and guide your way through the rest of the performance-appraisal process.

Conducting the Appraisal Meeting

This is the face-to-face meeting in which the manager and the employee discuss the employee's past job performance so the employee understands how he or she is doing, and agree on what needs to be done in the future to enhance current performance. The manager must guide this face-to-face meeting by asking appropriate questions and using effective listening skills. Later in this book, you'll learn the eight-step process for conducting an effective performance appraisal.

Following Up

Follow-up is essential to getting a return on the time and effort you've invested in preparing for and conducting the appraisal meeting. It ensures that employee commitments agreed to during the meeting are implemented, and that progress continues toward your mutually established goals. When follow-up becomes a part of the way you manage, you'll find that the human touch is truly an effective way to appraise employee performance.

Common Performance-Appraisal Problems

The human touch approach addresses many of the most common performance-appraisal problems. Think for a moment about the last few performance appraisals you conducted, then honestly answer "yes" or "no" to the questions below.

Yes No

1. Did you have frequent communication with your employees between appraisals?
2. Was there a close correlation between the employee's job description and the appraisal form you used?
3. Were there mutually agreed-to performance goals that came out of your meetings?
4. Did you evaluate your own performance before you evaluated your employees' performance?
5. Did you ask for others' input about your employees' performance?
6. Did you consistently document your employees' performance between appraisal meetings?
7. Were you well prepared for your appraisal meetings?
8. Did you prepare your employees for the appraisal meetings?
9. Did you have uninterrupted meetings?
10. Did you always ask for your employees' opinions?
11. Were you candid and specific about your employees' performance?
12. Did you remember to discuss your employees' positive accomplishments?
13. Did you focus on your employees' performance rather than on their personalities?
14. Did you close the appraisal meetings in a professional manner?
15. Did you follow up after the appraisal discussions?
16. Did you apply the human touch throughout the appraisal process?

If you answered "no" to any of these questions, don't feel bad. You're not alone. This book will address each of the 16 common performance-appraisal problems described above, as well as several other key aspects of the process. Throughout the book, you'll learn how to solve these common problems.

The Purposes and Benefits of Performance Appraisals

How do you feel when your boss says it's time for your performance appraisal? Do you react with fear? concern? excitement? enthusiasm? Whether it's your own performance that's being appraised or you're the one responsible for appraising an employee, performance appraisals never fail to bring out strong feelings—and usually they're feelings of dread.

One reason both managers and employees feel this way is that they don't understand the purposes and benefits of the appraisal process. Instead of approaching the appraisal in a positive manner, they focus on what they perceive to be the negatives. You may have heard (or even said) something like this:

◆ "I don't want to play God."

◆ "Human Resources just wants to make sure the paperwork is filled out."

◆ "It doesn't matter what I do, they only give so many 'superior' ratings."

◆ "Discussion? It always turns into an argument!"

When you understand the purposes and benefits of effective performance appraisals, you're bound to approach them with a more positive attitude.

Examine Employee Progress Toward Goals

Two-way communication is an essential part of the human touch.

Performance appraisals tell both the manager and the employee how much progress they're making toward meeting established goals. It also gives you as a manager an opportunity to reinforce the expectations you have for your employee. This two-way communication is an essential part of the human touch approach to performance appraisals.

The appraisal discussion also can help you find out if your employee is having problems. Since your job is to help your employee succeed, this information is critical. You can't afford to wait until it's too late to find out that things are off track.

From the other side of the table, the appraisal meeting gives your employees a chance to ask questions and tell you their sense of what they've accomplished. The two of you can discuss the steps planned to ensure that projects stay on course toward the desired goals, and review the status of key elements such as budgets and deadlines.

When it comes to employee performance, it's been said that "the best surprise is no surprise." Taking the time to discuss the progress toward meeting your goals keeps everyone informed so the outcomes won't be unexpected surprises. And the human touch lets managers help their employees successfully meet both their personal and professional goals.

Take a Moment

Yes No

☐ ☐ Are your employees working toward specific goals?

☐ ☐ Is their completed work meeting expectations?

☐ ☐ If not, are they aware that their work does not meet expectations?

☐ ☐ Are their projects on time and within budget?

☐ ☐ Have you given your employees help in meeting their goals?

☐ ☐ Is your greatest concern that your employees will be successful?

☐ ☐ Do your employees clearly understand exactly what is expected on the job?

If you answered "no" to any of the these questions, use the space below to jot down steps you can take to improve.

_____

_____

_____

Improving Employee Performance

If an employee is having problems meeting his or her goals, you can take steps during the appraisal to help improve performance. Perhaps you'll find that you need to provide additional information or resources. By working together, you and the employee should be able to ensure that mutual goals are indeed met.

The key is working together. Assume the role of a coach. Your employee still is responsible for meeting the agreed-upon goals; your capacity is to provide the help necessary for his or her performance to improve. Some managers fail at this point because, instead of coaching, they simply take over the task and do it themselves. These managers have succeeded only in increasing their own workload, not in encouraging improved employee performance.

Your role as a coach is an important part of the human touch appraisal process. As a coach, you can help your employee:

◆ Identify problems that may be affecting performance.

◆ Generate possible solutions, and map a plan to improve performance.

◆ Build on employee strengths.

You can use your experience and insight to help your employees identify the problems that are keeping them from meeting their goals. Ultimately, the success of your appraisal is measured by the degree to which the employee gains the knowledge and expertise needed to identify problems, generate possible solutions to them, and develop a plan to implement those solutions to improve performance.

When employee performance improves, the human touch performance-appraisal process has come full circle. How are you doing at helping your employees improve their performance?

Take a Moment

Yes No

☐   ☐ Do your employees have the resources they need?

☐   ☐ Do you help your employees solve their own problems?

☐   ☐ Do you help your employees generate a variety of solutions to their performance problems?

☐   ☐ Do you avoid taking on your employees' work?

If you answered "no" to any of the these questions, use the space below to jot down steps you can take to improve.

_____

_____

_____

Identify Current or Potential Problems

Sometimes employees will have problems that they're not even aware of. Or perhaps something they're doing now is likely to result in a problem down the road. In either case, your role is to help your employees identify these current or potential problems on their own.

The human touch performance-appraisal process gives you an opportunity to share your expertise about the ways things work in an organization, and the kinds of actions that can cause problems. Employees rarely do things wrong on purpose. They make mistakes because they lack knowledge, because they don't fully understand what is expected of them, or because they haven't considered alternative solutions to a problem.

When you fill in this missing information for them, you save both the employee and the organization valuable time. That's because in your role as a coach, you're filling in the "experience gap" so your employees can make better-informed decisions and improve their performance.

Manager's Level of Experience

Experience Gap

Employee's Level of Experience

One of the goals of the human touch process is to fill this experience gap and create more valuable employees for your organization.

Take a Moment

Yes No

☐ ☐ Are you aware of problems that your employees have right now, for which they need your help?

☐ ☐ Are your employees doing anything now that might result in a problem later?

☐ ☐ Do any of your employees have an experience gap?

☐ ☐ Do you have any experience gaps of your own?

If you answered "yes" to any of the these questions, use the space below to jot down steps you can take to improve.

_____

_____

_____

Making Employee-Manager Communication Frequent and Ongoing

We often think of performance appraisals as one-time events that take place every year or so. However, to be most effective, we should look at performance appraisals as an ongoing process. If you and your employees discuss performance only once a year, the time interval between meetings can allow problems to develop that seriously affect performance. Fortunately, the human touch appraisal process guarantees frequent two-way communication between you and your employees.

1

If you already meet with your employees to discuss their progress on a regular basis, you probably have employees who are meeting their goals. Holding frequent discussions shows your employees that you care about them and what they're doing—and is proof that you're applying the human touch.

Frequent communication also helps eliminate the needless uncertainty or worry that employees can experience when there is only minimal manager-employee interaction. When one of your employees seldom hears from you, he or she may develop doubts about the acceptability of his or her performance. When you use the human touch, you talk to your employees often, automatically relieving these doubts.

Common Performance-Appraisal Problem #1: Lack of Frequent Communication

SOLUTION:
Frequent communication provides the opportunity for both you and your employee to check perceptions against reality. When both of you have an accurate understanding of what the other person is thinking, communication and performance both improve.

Take a Moment

Yes No

☐ ☐ Do you frequently communicate with your employees?

☐ ☐ Have you taken steps to remove any obstacles that may be limiting employee performance?

☐ ☐ Do your employees feel free to ask you questions?

☐ ☐ Do your perceptions of your employees' performance match theirs?

If you answered "no" to any of the these questions, use the space below to jot down steps you can take to improve.

_____

_____

_____

Some Perspectives on Performance Appraisals

A Historical View

One of the earliest recorded efforts at appraising job performance occurred in the U.S. Army. In 1813, General Lewis Cass was asked to provide a formal evaluation of his men. Although General Cass's comments provide a humorous example, they also identify the problem that occurs when there are no specific goals established against which to evaluate performance.

- This officer has talents but has kept them well hidden.

- Does not drink, but is a good mixer.

- Can express a sentence in two paragraphs at a time.

- He has failed to demonstrate any outstanding weaknesses.

- Open to suggestions, but never follows same.

- An exceptionally well-qualified officer.

- Of average intelligence, except for lack of judgment on one occasion, in attempting to capture a rattlesnake for which he was hospitalized.[1]

Despite the obvious drawbacks of such a "trait" rating system, the U.S. military continued to be in the forefront of developing a standardized appraisal process. In the 1800s, other federal institutions, such as Congress and the Civil Service, attempted to implement performance-evaluation systems with varying degrees of success.

The best way to evaluate performance is to focus on the employee's behaviors and results.

The first formal evaluation process in private business is thought to have been initiated in 1913 by Lord & Taylor, a New York City department store. Following World War I, many businesses adopted various merit systems of performance evaluation. Most tended to focus on the traits of the employee and how he or she approached the job, rather than on the results of their performance.

[1] Thomas H. Patten, Jr. *Pay: Employee Compensation and Incentive Plans* (New York: The Free Press, 1977), p. 337.

Over the years, both government and business have tried various systems to come up with "the" way to evaluate performance. It now has become generally accepted that the best way to evaluate performance is to focus on the employee's behaviors and results—not on their personality traits. Performance appraisals have become the preferred method for observing, evaluating, and measuring employee performance.

It is estimated that perhaps only one-half of the large organizations in America have formal appraisal systems for salaried employees, and that virtually none of the millions of smaller businesses do.[2]

Salary Administration and Performance Appraisals

Often the review of an employee's performance is tied to his or her salary. This system usually is referred to as "pay for performance." When it's time to determine how much of a raise, if any, an employee will receive, the performance appraisal becomes the determining factor. The better the performance, the greater the raise—at least, that's the underlying assumption. On the surface, pay for performance sounds good, but there can be several problems when pay increases depend on the outcome of the appraisal meeting.

First, there is the tendency of the employee to want to discuss examples of stellar performance and to explain away anything that might negatively affect the increase. The meeting can turn into a battle of explanations between manager and employee, rather than an open discussion of performance and how it can be improved.

Another problem is that company budgets or personnel policies often dictate the amount of increase a manager can give an employee or a group of employees. A manager may have to face the fact that business conditions or national cost-of-living figures impose a limit on the raises he or she can give. In such cases, even though an employee's performance may be better than the previous year, the amount of the increase may be lower. This can weaken employee morale and, as a result, future performance.

[2] Thomas H. Patten, Jr. *A Manager's Guide to Performance Appraisal* (New York: The Free Press, 1982), p. 11.

Many experts now recommend cutting the ties between salary increases and performance appraisals.

When the issue of salary becomes the focus of the appraisal meeting and not the employee's performance, the benefits of the human touch performance appraisal discussed earlier are quickly lost. Even though salary considerations may not be mentioned directly, they're on everyone's mind throughout the discussion.

To defuse this conflict, many experts now recommend cutting the ties between salary increases and performance appraisals. One way to do this is with two separate discussions—one focused on pay and one focused on performance. This allows the manager and employee to openly discuss performance without the specter of salary looming overhead. Then when it's time to discuss pay raises, both parties have the same focus for the meeting.

If your organization is one that ties performance to pay increases, all is not lost. Pay-for-performance also has its share of supporters. They argue that, if you measure performance as accurately and objectively as possible, you can and should use it to determine the amount of a pay increase.

The key to making either system work is for managers to demonstrate that they are concerned about their employees' needs, wants, expectations, and goals—in short, to use the human touch. Managers who use the human touch process are communicating that, although salary is important, in the long run, it's the way you treat your employees on a daily basis that determines their real success.

Your Perspective

If your organization has a formal appraisal system:

◆ Do you understand the system?

◆ Does the system focus on employee behavior and results, or on personality traits?

◆ Is it a pay-for-performance system?

◆ If so, are pay and appraisals handled in separate discussions?

If you answered "I don't know" to any of these questions, use the space below to list steps you can take to learn the answers.

_____

_____

_____

_____

Self-Check: Chapter 1 Review

Now that you've read Chapter 1, use this space to review what you've learned so far. If you're not sure of an answer, just refer to the text. Answers appear on page 90.

1. What are the three steps of the human touch performance-appraisal process?

    a. _____

    b. _____

    c. _____

2. Briefly describe what it means to apply the human touch.

    _____

    _____

    _____

    _____

    _____

    _____

    _____

    _____

3. What are the purposes and benefits of performance appraisals?

    a. _____

    b. _____

    c. _____

    d. _____

1

4. Where did the idea of appraising performance originate?

_____

_____

_____

_____

5. What are the disadvantages of linking pay increases to performance appraisals?

_____

_____

_____

_____

_____

_____

_____

6. What can you do to make a pay-for-performance appraisal system work in your organization?

_____

_____

_____

_____

_____

_____

Chapter *Two*

Preparing for the Appraisal Meeting

Chapter Objectives

▶ Describe the personnel-management cycle.

▶ List the requirements for effective performance appraisals.

▶ Set goals with your employees.

▶ Prepare to conduct an appraisal discussion.

The human touch performance-appraisal system takes into account the relationship among the employee's job description, ongoing feedback about performance and how additional training can improve it, and the performance-appraisal meeting. We can view this relationship as a cyclical process: the personnel-management cycle.

The Personnel-Management Cycle

The personnel-managment cycle consists of three parts, as illustrated by the diagram on the following page:

1. The job description

2. Ongoing feedback and training

3. The performance appraisal

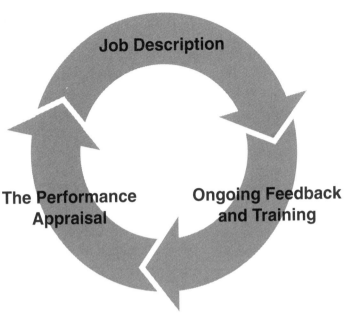

Job Description

Ongoing Feedback and Training

The Performance Appraisal

2

The *job description* should be an accurate reflection of what is expected of the employee. Often, job descriptions are not kept up to date, and they describe duties that are unnecessary or that are no longer being performed. Jobs change, and so do the people performing them. That's why job descriptions should be updated annually. An accurate and current job description is the best vehicle for telling your employee exactly what is expected on the job.

The more specific the job description, the easier it will be to set goals with the employee. These goals then form the basis of the performance-appraisal discussion. A well-written job description can also help you identify the training you need to provide your employee.

If you don't have current job descriptions, take time to develop them for all of your people. One of the best ways to develop job descriptions is to conduct a meeting of several people who perform the same job. Ask them to list all their duties, then organize the list into categories with related items, as was done in the sample job description on page 27. You also should involve the person who supervises the job; he or she may identify additional duties to add, or some to delete.

> **The more specific the job description, the easier it will be to set goals with the employee.**

The time you spend putting together job descriptions and developing goals will enhance the human touch appraisal process. Unless the relationship between the job description and the appraisal form is obvious to both the manager and the employee, there's always the likelihood that performance may be evaluated on non-job-related items.

For example, suppose one of the items on an employee's job description was "prepares and submits weekly activity reports." During the employee's training, the manager would be expected to teach the employee the correct way to prepare and submit these activity reports. This training phase of the personnel-management cycle should cover everything the employee needs to know about weekly activity reports—how to prepare them, when to turn them in, and to whom.

A performance-appraisal form should replay the exact language of the job description.

The performance-appraisal form should replay the exact language of the job description, thus completing the cycle. During the appraisal discussion, the manager and the employee should talk about how well the employee "prepares and submits weekly activity reports." And the evaluation should be based on the specific goals and expectations for preparing and submitting activity reports that the manager and employee already have discussed and agreed upon.

If the employee's performance does not meet standards and training is the problem, it's the manager's responsibility to provide that training. One of the benefits of the human touch approach is that it helps identify areas in which training has been insufficient, and ensures that your people get whatever training is necessary for them to improve their performance. It's yet another way to demonstrate that you care about your employees and you want to see them succeed.

JOB DESCRIPTION

___ Original
___ Revised

Job Title: _____

Department: _____

Supervisor's Title: _____

2

Position Summary and Essential Functions:

Provides administrative support to operations staff, including typing correspondence, contracts, etc.; making travel arrangements; coordinating meetings; assisting with budget tracking; and answering phones.

Responsibilities:

1. Types all correspondence, proposals, contracts, etc. Ensures that documents are produced with high quality and within established time frames.

2. Coordinates travel arrangements for operations department, utilizing the in-house agency. Prepares itineraries, travel advances, and reimbursement requests in compliance with Company policy.

3. Schedules meetings by coordinating and confirming attendance, arranging for meeting place, equipment, etc.

4. Maintains budgetary tracking system and reports deviations to the vice president.

5. Prepares purchase requisitions in conformity with Company policy, and ensures that vendor files and bills are timely.

6. Answers phone for vice president and other staff members as necessary. Provides a high level of customer service.

7. Other duties as assigned.

Education and Experience:

1. High school graduate or equivalent work experience.

2. Secretarial/administrative education helpful.

3. Three years secretarial/administrative experience preferred.

Knowledge, Skills, Abilities, and Physical Requirements:

1. Must be able to type 60 words per minute.

2. Knowledge of WordPerfect and Lotus 1-2-3 helpful.

3. Ability to communicate effectively (written and oral).

4. Knowledge in office administration, follow-up systems, preparation of purchase requisitions, and scheduling facilities.

5. Knowledge of Company helpful.

Take a Moment

Relating the Job Description to Performance-Appraisal Goals

Using the sample job description on page 27, develop three goals or standards for the position.

1. _____

_____

2. _____

_____

3. _____

_____

Based on these goals, what would be discussed in the appraisal meeting?

_____

_____

_____

_____

_____

Common Performance-Appraisal Problem #2: Job Description and Performace Appraisal Aren't Related

SOLUTION:
Establishing and maintaining a direct relationship between the job description and the performance-appraisal form helps keep you and your employees focused on the same set of job expectations throughout the performance-appraisal process.

Take a Moment

How's Your Personnel-Management Cycle?

Yes   No

❑   ❑   Do you have accurate and current job descriptions for all of your employees?

If not, what steps do you need to take to update them?

_____

_____

❑   ❑   Is your training designed to teach employees how to do the tasks outlined in their job descriptions?

If not, how can you change the training?

_____

_____

❑   ❑   Is the relationship among the job description (including its goals and expectations), training, and the performance appraisal clear to both you and your employees?

If not, what changes need to be made?

_____

_____

What's your time frame for making any needed changes listed above?

_____

_____

2

Requirements of the Human Touch Performance Appraisal

If you're going to have an effective one-on-one discussion with your employee—one that's beneficial to both of you—your performance appraisal needs to meet these five requirements:

1. Measure Progress and Ability

The human touch appraisal must measure the progress your employee has made against predetermined goals. It's also important to discuss how well the employee has applied his or her abilities to performing the job. The discussion should answer questions such as:

◆ Could more progress have been made with more effort?

◆ Was the employee working at full capacity in trying to meet his or her goals?

◆ Is the employee's progress acceptable, in light of any unforeseen obstacles that may have affected results?

2. Tie the Appraisal to the Employee's Job

Stick to the goals and expectations found in the job description.

The human touch appraisal needs to stay focused on the requirements spelled out in the job description. Don't surprise the employee during the discussion by using non-job-related criteria to evaluate performance. For example, you might have an employee who occasionally devotes time to volunteer activities during the workday, but who always works extra hours to compensate for any missed work. Unless you or your organization specifically prohibits such an arrangement, the volunteer activities shouldn't be a factor in the performance appraisal.

3. Be Objective

Establish goals on a regular basis to help ensure that performance appraisals will be objective. The more objective the appraisal, the less likely there are to be disagreements about the employee's level of performance. For example, if the employee had a goal to attain a 10 percent sales increase and only achieved 5 percent, you can talk objectively about performance. On the other hand, if the goal had simply been stated as "to increase sales," then, technically, any increase would meet it. An objective appraisal enables both parties to come away from the face-to-face meeting feeling good about what was discussed.

4. Build on Your Employee's Strengths

The human touch appraisal discussion should provide feedback on the employee's past results and give him or her guidance for the future. Make it a point to focus on what the employee has done well. Build on strengths, and give positive feedback to encourage the employee to maintain or improve performance. Once again, letting the employee know that you recognize and appreciate his or her strengths shows that you care. Building on strengths is one of the best ways to put the human touch in action.

If there are problems here, spend time on developing a corrective-action plan that the employee can use to improve current levels of performance. Just don't let the time spent discussing corrective action overshadow your review of all the positive contributions the employee has been making to the organization. Dwelling on weaknesses can paralyze your people.

Make it a point to focus on what the employee has done well.

5. Meet Legal Requirements

The Equal Employment Opportunity Commission (EEOC) requires that any measurement used to differentiate between employees must be valid and fairly administered. The Americans with Disabilities Act (ADA) suggests that performance appraisals for people with disabilities will not be conducted any differently than those for other employees. That's why it's important for the appraisal to focus on the requirements listed in the employee's job description. Having specific goals also helps ensure that the appraisal does not focus on areas that could be considered discriminatory.

How well your performance appraisals meet these five requirements also will determine how effective they'll be in supporting your organization's personnel decisions and how legally defensible your personnel decisions will be if they're ever contested in a court of law. This doesn't mean you have to be a lawyer. It does mean that you should do everything possible to develop an objective performance-appraisal system that does not discriminate against any employee.

Take a Moment

Are You Meeting Requirements?

Take a proactive approach when you plan for the appraisal discussion. Use the space below to jot down specific actions you can take to meet the five performance-appraisal requirements just discussed.

How will you measure your employee's progress in meeting goals?

_____

_____

_____

How will you ensure that the appraisal is tied to the employee's job?

_____

_____

_____

What will you do to remain objective?

_____

_____

_____

How will you be constructive?

_____

_____

_____

What will you do to ensure that your appraisals meet legal requirements?

_____

_____

_____

Setting Goals

The human touch appraisal process will be successful only if you and your employee set performance goals. And you need to do this together, so there's mutual agreement about what the employee is expected to accomplish. The communication between you and your employee at this point in the process sets the stage for everything that will happen right up until the time of the formal appraisal discussion. Without previously agreed-upon goals, it will be difficult, if not impossible, to evaluate performance, and the appraisal discussion easily can wind up being more of an argument about who was supposed to do what, for whom, and by when.

2

Criteria for Setting Goals

- **Specify the desired result.** What task will be accomplished if the goal is achieved?

- **Make the result measurable.** Can you differentiate among different degrees of achievement?

- **Set a time frame.** By what date must this goal be achieved?

- **Discuss any cost considerations.** How much, if anything, will achieving this goal cost in terms of money and resources? Are there specific budget guidelines that must be adhered to?

For example: "Establish an appraisal system that includes job descriptions, training, and an appraisal form that specifies goals and expectations by June 15 at a cost not to exceed $5,000."

Here's how this statement meets our four criteria:

- **The specific result:** "Establish an appraisal system . . ." describes the overall result we're looking for.

- **Measurability:** ". . . that includes job descriptions, training, and an appraisal form that specifies goals and expectations . . ." are qualitative measures that specify in even greater detail what the appraisal system will look like.

Goal Criteria:
- ◆ Specific task
- ◆ Measurable outcome
- ◆ Time frame
- ◆ Cost considerations

◆ **Time frame:** ". . . by June 15 . . ." tells when it will be completed.

◆ **Cost considerations:** ". . . and at a cost not to exceed $5,000" specifies how much money is available to invest in the project. These last two criteria also are measures—but they're quantitative measures, which are easier to evaluate: either the result was accomplished on time and on budget, or it wasn't.

In addition to meeting these four criteria, goals also must be realistic yet challenging. Although the previous goal contains all the appropriate criteria, if it were drafted on June 1, it may not be realistic. In fact, it may be downright impossible if the employee has several other projects. People quickly lose their enthusiasm if they believe that they are expected to achieve impossible goals. That's why the human touch approach asks you to set goals in consultation with your employees. That way, you'll both agree that the goals you arrive at will be the ones that should be used to evaluate performance.

Goals must be written down. Just talking about them isn't enough.

Goals must be written down. Just talking about them isn't enough. When you take the time to write down your goals, you're making a commitment to yourself that they're important. Having your goals in writing also makes it easier to check them against the four criteria. Working with your employees to develop written goals is still another way to demonstrate to them that you care about their success. Be sure to write down your goals, and be sure that both you and your employee have copies so they're mutually understood.

Common Performance-Appraisal Problem #3: No Mutually Agreed-Upon Goals

SOLUTION:
Involving the employee in goal-setting ensures that they'll "buy in" to the level of performance the manager expects. That way, there isn't any surprise at appraisal time. The employee can't say, "I didn't know what you wanted," and the manager can't say, "That wasn't what I wanted." Establishing goals up front and then writing them down helps take the guesswork out of the appraisal process and creates an opportunity to apply the human touch.

Take a Moment

Identifying and Writing Good Performance Goals

Identify the four goal criteria in the following statement: "Develop a four-part form for documenting employee performance that can be implemented company-wide by January 1 with printing and distribution costs not to exceed $575."

Suggested responses are on page 91.

1. What's the task to be accomplished?

   _____

   _____

2. What will it look like when it is completed?

   _____

   _____

3. When must it be completed?

   _____

4. What are the cost considerations?

   _____

5. Revise the goal statements below so they meet the four criteria of addressing a specific task, measurable outcome, time frame, and cost considerations.

   "Improve the quality of communication between our employees and customers."

   _____

   _____

   "Decrease the number of complaints from customers."

   _____

   _____

2

Once you and your employees have established and written down your goals, you can use them to measure your progress on a regular basis—not just during the formal performance appraisal. Since you both know what's expected, if either of you sees indications that your goals may not be attained, you can request a meeting to discuss corrective action. This is one way that you, as a manager, can help fill experience gaps your employee may have and help him or her get back on track toward meeting goals.

Preparing to Conduct an Appraisal Discussion

Approximately two weeks before the appraisal meeting, you should begin preparing for it by taking these five steps:

1. Evaluating your own performance

2. Involving others

3. Gathering any helpful documentation

4. Preparing yourself for the appraisal discussion

5. Preparing the employee

Begin with a candid evaluation of your own performance.

Evaluating Your Own Performance

The human touch performance-appraisal process begins with a candid evaluation of your own performance. Since your performance can affect your employee's performance, it's important to take this step before you evaluate the performance of others.

Take a Moment

Yes No

☐ ☐ Have you and the employee set mutually agreed-upon goals?

☐ ☐ Have you provided regular feedback on the employee's performance since the last formal appraisal?

☐ ☐ Are you aware of any obstacles that have prevented the employee from meeting his or her goals?

☐ ☐ Have you provided assistance to help the employee meet his or her goals?

☐ ☐ Has the employee willingly come to you with questions?

☐ ☐ Has your own performance served as a role model for the employee?

☐ ☐ If any of your goals that affect the employee have changed, have you informed the employee?

Make a note of anything about your own performance that you think you may need to consider when evaluating your employees' performance.

_____

_____

_____

Common Performance-Appraisal Problem #4: Failure to Evaluate Your Own Performance First

SOLUTION:
Take time to evaluate your own performance before you evaluate the performance of those who work for you. There may be things you are or are not doing that are affecting your employees' performance. Make sure that what you are doing supports the efforts of your employees to reach their goals.

Involving Others

Although the appraisal discussion will focus on the goals you and your employee have set together, it's still a good idea to get input from others who may have insight into the employee's performance.

◆ **The employee's peers**
As organization structures become flatter, managers often have several employees whose performance they have to appraise. Peer review allows you to obtain an evaluation from colleagues who have knowledge of the employee's performance to aid you in your own review. In order for such a system to work, there must be established goals. Otherwise, a peer review can turn into a popularity—or unpopularity—contest.

A peer review can have other drawbacks as well. It will take extra time to gather input from several people. It can be hard to keep peer input confidential. And sometimes evaluators tend to remember isolated incidents or to blow them out of proportion—both favorable and unfavorable examples. However, if the manager is aware of these drawbacks, he or she can take steps to prevent them from having a negative impact. The key to a successful peer review is to keep the evaluators focused on how well the employee met established goals rather than on his or her personality.

◆ **Your boss**
In many organizations, any appraisal rating must be approved by at least two levels of management. So it makes sense to discuss the appraisal with your boss ahead of time. This provides you with an opportunity to get another perspective on the employee's performance. And it protects you from making promises or commitments to the employee during the appraisal discussion that you later discover your boss won't support.

Normally there will be a relationship between your own goals and those you establish with your employee, just as there should be between your goals and those of your boss and the entire organization. By meeting with your boss ahead of time, you have an opportunity to get feedback on your own performance. This information can help you see if you've been giving your employees adequate support in meeting their goals.

2

**Common Performance-Appraisal Problem #5:
Not Obtaining Input from Others About
the Employee's Performance**

SOLUTION:
The more people you involve in the review process, the more information you'll have with which to make informed decisions about the employee's performance. Be sure the input you get from others is focused on established goals and not on the employee's personality.

◆ **Other employees**
People in other parts of the organization who have worked with your employee but who are not considered peers can be valuable sources of information. For example, a person in a staff position, such as research and development, may interact with people in a variety of other departments.

By talking to others who have worked with your employee, you can get an idea of how the employee interacts with others and presents him- or herself in other parts of the organization. This information can be extremely valuable in organizations where teamwork among various departments is valued. You may find that the employee has certain strengths that you aren't taking advantage of, or weaknesses that need to be addressed.

Take a Moment

Whom Can You Involve?

Use this space to identfy people you want to involve when you prepare for appraisal discussions with your employees.

Peers

_____

_____

_____

Your manager(s)

_____

_____

_____

Other employees

_____

_____

_____

Gathering Any Helpful Documentation

Once you and your employee have established your goals, you should maintain ongoing written documentation of the results the employee achieves. Sometimes the word _documentation_ has the negative connotation that what's being documented are all instances of poor performance to be placed in the employee's personnel file. Quite the contrary; the human touch performance-appraisal process asks you to document positive results as well.

Document good performance as well as bad.

Documenting employee performance throughout the year helps you conduct an accurate and effective appraisal discussion. Without such documentation, you may tend to emphasize just one example of employee performance during the appraisal period. For example, an employee might have done a spectacular job on one high-visibility project, but only an average job on everything else. Without more comprehensive documentation, you may award a rating that is higher than it really should be. The opposite could also occur. When documenting performance, it's important to be specific. For example, "Great job on the budget!" won't tell you much at appraisal time. A more specific description might include comments such as:

- "Analyzed last year's budget first."

- "Talked to other departments."

- "Suggested ways to streamline the process."

The manager who applies the human touch doesn't rely on memory when it's time to conduct an appraisal interview.

It's better to have too much detail than not enough. The manager who applies the human touch doesn't rely on memory when it's time to conduct an appraisal discussion.

There are several sources of information that can help you as you document employee performance:

- Written reports submitted by the employee; some organizations require weekly or monthly activity reports.

- Financial statements that reflect the employee's performance.

- Copies of correspondence that you or the employee have received.

- Personal notes you've written based on your observation of the employee's results.

- Personal notes that document comments from others who have worked with the employee.

- Training courses the employee has taken.

- Notes regarding any disciplinary action you have taken.

- Noteworthy successes or failures.

Note: Following the appraisal discussion, start a new file for the coming appraisal period. This will prevent future performance appraisals from being affected by results (positive or negative) that were achieved during previous appraisal periods. Remember that in most states, you have to maintain employee records for three years. So just move past years' employee records; don't throw them away.

Take a Moment

How's Your Documentation?

Use this space to list several sources of employee documentation that you plan to use during the next appraisal period.

_____

_____

_____

_____

Common Performance-Appraisal Problem #6: Not Documenting Performance Between Appraisal Discussions

SOLUTION:

The key to using documentation effectively is to draw on as many sources as possible, and to maintain your own ongoing, consistent documentation throughout the appraisal period. It's just as important to document examples of superior performance as it is to note times when performance didn't meet expectations.

Take a Moment

Employee Documentation

Here are five good/bad examples of employee documentation. Mark "yes" if the documentation is proper, and "no" if it is not. Answers appear on page 91.

Yes No

❑   ❑   Joe was late for work three times last week.

❑   ❑   Joe's reports are always late.

❑   ❑   On 9/16, Joe failed to replace the safety shield on machine 43 before re-engaging.

❑   ❑   Joe's production level was 17 percent above written performance standards for January.

❑   ❑   I saw Joe helping someone from shipping.

Preparing Yourself for the Appraisal Discussion

An important part of applying the human touch is to prepare yourself for the appraisal discussion. The better prepared you are, the better the discussion will be. Your preparation also will help keep the meeting focused and ensure that it achieves the results you want. Here are some questions you should ask yourself when preparing for a human touch performance appraisal:

2

◆ What results do I want from this appraisal?

◆ What contribution is this employee making?

◆ What contribution should the employee be making?

◆ Is the employee working near his or her potential?

◆ Does the employee know exactly what level of performance is expected?

◆ What training, if any, does this employee need?

◆ What are this employee's strengths?

◆ How has my performance helped or hindered my employee in achieving his or her goals?

◆ What action can I take to help?

Once you answer these questions for yourself, you'll be in a better position to finish preparing for the upcoming discussion. Employees always can tell whether or not you've taken the time to prepare for the appraisal meeting. And preparation demonstrates to your people that you've invested time to make your discussions meaningful.

Build on your employee's strengths.

It probably can't be overemphasized: A key part of the performance appraisal is the opportunity to build on your employee's strengths. The manager can acknowledge the employee's strengths and past contributions and encourage future development. To prepare for your discussion, list your employee's strengths and how they're important to the job. It's helpful to ask others in your organization for feedback as well. Make your list available for review during your appraisal discussion.

Use the following Take a Moment exercise to determine your readiness for conducting a human touch appraisal discussion.

Take a Moment

Yes No

☐ ☐ Have you evaluated your own performance as it relates to your employee's performance?

☐ ☐ Have you asked for any needed peer reviews?

☐ ☐ Have you reviewed the appraisal with your boss and obtained agreement on the rating?

☐ ☐ Have you asked others who have worked with the employee for their input?

☐ ☐ Have you gathered all possible documentation regarding the employee's performance?

☐ ☐ Do you have a copy of the mutually agreed-to goals?

☐ ☐ Do you have a copy of the employee's up-to-date job description?

☐ ☐ Have you set a date, time, and place for a private meeting?

☐ ☐ Have you given the employee a copy of the appraisal form?

☐ ☐ Have you given the employee the opportunity to ask questions about the appraisal process?

☐ ☐ Are you prepared to compare the employee's performance to your established goals?

If you answered "no" to any of these questions, use the space below to list the actions you need to take to prepare for the appraisal discussion.

_____

_____

Common Performance-Appraisal Problem #7:
Not Preparing for the Discussion

SOLUTION:
The human touch performance-appraisal process requires a commitment on your part to prepare for the discussion. If you just walk into the meeting room and "wing it," you'll send the wrong message to your employee. Start preparing and organizing at least two weeks prior to the discussion so you'll be able to accurately evaluate your employee's performance.

2

Preparing the Employee

The human touch appraisal process focuses on involving the employee as much as possible. There are several things you can do to prepare the employee for the upcoming appraisal:

- Set a date, time, and place. Consult with the employee and find out when he or she is available to meet.

- Send the employee written confirmation of the meeting date, time, and place. Be sure to explain the purpose of the discussion and how the results will be used. Give the employee the same professional courtesy you would accord any business associate.

- Make sure the employee has a copy of the goals and the appraisal form that will be used at the meeting.

- Give the employee the opportunity to ask questions. Consider holding a "briefing" meeting with the employee to cover all of these topics and to find out if the employee has any questions or concerns before the actual appraisal discussion.

- Ask the employee to evaluate his or her own performance before the discussion, and be prepared to defend the evaluation.

> Make sure the employee has a copy of the goals and the appraisal form that will be used at the meeting.

Common Performance-Appraisal Problem #8:
Not Preparing the Employee for the Discussion

SOLUTION:
Demonstrate that you care about the employee by telling him or her well in advance when the appraisal will be and how to prepare for the meeting. The more involved the employee is in the whole process, the better.

Self-Check: Chapter 2 Review

Preparation is critical to your success with the human touch performance-appraisal process. Answer the following questions to evaluate your understanding of how to prepare for the appraisal discussion. If you're not sure of an answer, just refer to the text. Answers appear on pages 91 and 92.

1. What three items make up the personnel-management cycle?

    a. _____

    b. _____

    c. _____

2. What are the requirements for an effective one-on-one appraisal discussion?

    a. _____

    b. _____

    c. _____

    d. _____

    e. _____

3. Finish the statements below about the four criteria that goals should meet.

    They should be _____ and state what is to be accomplished.

    They should be _____ so you can describe what the results will look like.

    They should specify a definite _____ frame.

    Any _____ also should be included.

4. Why is it important to evaluate your own performance before the appraisal discussion?

    _____

    _____

    _____

5. List three groups you might involve in obtaining feedback
    about your employee's performance.

    a. _____

    b. _____

    c. _____

2

6. List four kinds of information you could include as
    documentation.

    a. _____

    b. _____

    c. _____

    d. _____

7. What should you do to prepare your employee for the
    appraisal discussion?

    _____

    _____

    _____

    _____

    _____

    _____

Chapter *Three*

Conducting the Appraisal Discussion

Chapter Objectives

▶ Describe the characteristics of an effective performance-appraisal discussion leader.

▶ Follow the eight-step appraisal-discussion process.

The human touch performance appraisal helps create a climate of motivation. When you care about your employees, are genuinely interested in their ideas and opinions, and are willing to listen to them, you can develop a motivating climate throughout the appraisal process.

Characteristics of an Effective Discussion Leader

Your success in the appraisal process depends on your skills as a discussion leader.

Much of your success in the appraisal process depends on your skills as a discussion leader. An effective discussion leader provides an opportunity for the other person to explain his or her views and works to keep the channels of communication open. When the appraisal discussion is over, both parties should have a better understanding of each other and how their job performances are related.

Take a Moment

The characteristics below describe what an effective discussion leader must be able to do during the appraisal process. Circle the number that best represents where you think you are on the scale. When you are finished, write your score in the space provided. Be honest with yourself.

Poor Average Excellent

1	2	3	4	5	I sincerely care about my employees.
1	2	3	4	5	I am concerned when my employees don't succeed.
1	2	3	4	5	I encourage my employees to come to me with problems.
1	2	3	4	5	My employees feel free to come and talk with me about almost anything.
1	2	3	4	5	I give positive feedback whenever possible.
1	2	3	4	5	I can give corrective feedback when necessary.
1	2	3	4	5	I want my employees to tell me what they think.
1	2	3	4	5	I can listen to people without interrupting.
1	2	3	4	5	I like being responsible for other people.
1	2	3	4	5	I pay attention to the needs of my employees.
1	2	3	4	5	I know what training and development resources are available for my employees.
1	2	3	4	5	I always have a positive and caring attitude toward my employees.

Total Score: _____

A score between 48 and 60 indicates that you have the characteristics needed to be an effective discussion leader. If you scored 36 to 47, you have a solid base on which to build. Take a look at any items that you rated as 3 or below. These may indicate opportunities for improvement. But regardless of your score, as you work through this chapter, look for ways to sharpen your skills and build on your strengths.

3

The Eight-Step Appraisal-Discussion Process

The best way to control the time and the quality of the discussion is to plan it. This chapter breaks the discussion process down into eight manageable steps:

Step 1: Control the environment.

Step 2: State the purpose of the discussion.

Step 3: Ask for the employee's opinion.

Step 4: Present your assessment.

Step 5: Build on the employee's strengths.

Step 6: Ask for the employee's reaction to your assessment.

Step 7: Set specific goals.

Step 8: Close the discussion.

If you take the time to develop a discussion plan around these eight steps, you'll find that your appraisal discussions can be more meaningful and productive.

The total time spent in the appraisal discussion should be approximately one hour. If the discussion is shorter, you probably won't be able to cover everything you need to discuss. On the other hand, if it's much longer, it may be because you haven't stayed on track and the discussion has wandered.

Step 1: Control the Environment

One of the ways to put the human touch to work is in the way you control the environment of the appraisal discussion. Schedule the meeting for a time when you won't be interrupted. It's often a good idea to hold the meeting somewhere other than in your office—a conference room, perhaps—to reduce the potential for interruptions by visitors or phone calls. Your entire focus should be on the employee and his or her performance.

> The best way to control the time and the quality of the discussion is to plan it.

> Your entire focus should be on the employee and his or her performance.

**Common Performance-Appraisal Problem #9:
Allowing Interruptions During the Discussion**

SOLUTION:
The human touch appraisal process requires giving your full attention to the employee during the discussion. If you allow interruptions during the meeting, you are communicating to your employee that there are more important things than this discussion. The employee may think that his or her performance results don't matter that much to you.

3

The Warm-Up

One way to control the environment is to begin the appraisal discussion with a warm-up. This will demonstrate to the employee that you care. The goal of the warm-up is to set the stage for the rest of the discussion.

Put the employee at ease.

Put the employee at ease so you can reduce any fear or tension that he or she might have. As mentioned in the previous chapter, take time to schedule the discussion in advance and inform the employee when the discussion will be conducted. Remember to make sure that the employee has copies of his or her performance goals and job description (it's best if they're combined on the same document) and a copy of the appraisal form so he or she can complete a self-evaluation prior to the meeting. These steps will go a long way toward reducing the employee's anxiety before the discussion.

Another way is to plan your opening remarks. If you were conducting a staff meeting with your employees, you would plan what you were going to say at the outset. The same holds true for the appraisal discussion. Don't run into the meeting room at the last minute unsure of what you're going to say.

Planning opening remarks doesn't mean that you have to write a script. You might, however, make a few notes to yourself about things you want to talk about at the outset and write out a sequence. For example, you might want to ask a question about something other than work. Let the employee know that you care about him or her as a person—not just as an employee.

This is another opportunity to apply the human touch to the discussion. However, only make a nonbusiness comment if you already do this on a daily basis. Otherwise, you may appear to be insincere.

Step 2: State the Purpose of the Discussion

Go over the advantages of the appraisal discussion.

Once the warm-up is over, but before you begin to review the employee's performance, state the purpose of the discussion. If you have properly prepared the employee, he or she already should know the purpose. But reiterating it serves to reinforce for the employee that there hasn't been a change in plans.

You also can demonstrate the human touch by going over the advantages of the appraisal discussion, and the ways it will let both of you:

◆ Discuss progress toward goals.

◆ Identify ways to improve performance.

◆ Identify current or potential problems.

◆ Improve communication.

When the employee understands the purposes and advantages of the appraisal process, it's easier to have an effective discussion.

This also is a good time to tell the employee what information you will be using to evaluate his or her performance, such as:

◆ Established goals

◆ Your own performance

◆ Input from others

◆ The employee's input

◆ Written documentation

◆ Results

Take a Moment

How Will You Prepare for the Discussion?

Take a moment now to evaluate your readiness to complete the first two steps in the appraisal discussion.

How will you control the environment?

_____

_____

How will you put your employee at ease?

_____

_____

What do you plan to say at the outset?

_____

_____

What are the advantages to the employee of this discussion?

_____

_____

What information will you use to evaluate the employee's performance?

_____

_____

What else will you do to start this discussion off right?

_____

_____

3

Step 3: Ask for the Employee's Opinion

There is disagreement among the "experts" as to whether or not you should present your assessment (Step 4) before you ask for the employee's opinion. Some believe that you should state your position first, so the employee knows what you think before you ask for his or her opinion. These experts believe that this puts the manager in a stronger position during the discussion that follows.

This "expert" believes in asking for the employee's opinion first as another way of demonstrating the human touch. During the preparation phase, you asked the employee to rate his or her own performance. Presumably, you did this without previewing your own assessment. Asking the employee to present his or her evaluation first shows that you care and are just as interested in what he or she thinks as you are in your own evaluation.

Common Performance-Appraisal Problem #10: Not Asking for the Employee's Opinion

SOLUTION:
During the human touch appraisal discussion, the employee should do most of the talking about his or her performance. Throughout the discussion, ask for the employee's opinion regarding his or her performance. This will give you insight into how the employee views his or her performance, strengths, and opportunities for improvement. Knowing the employee's opinion puts you in a better position to provide any needed assistance.

One of the best ways to get employees to open up is to ask questions and then to actively listen to their answers.

Employees sometimes are reluctant to open up during the appraisal discussion. You can increase their willingness to participate by creating an atmosphere that communicates your interest in them and in what they have to say. One of the best ways to get employees to open up is to ask questions and then to actively listen to their answers.

Getting the employee to open up depends in part on your ability to ask the right kinds of questions. Effective discussion leaders use two types of questions:

◆ Open-ended questions

◆ Closed-ended questions

Open-Ended Questions

Open-ended questions cannot be answered with a simple yes or no. They are intended to get the employee to open up and share his or her opinions and feelings. They typically begin with words like "who," "what," "when," "where," "why," and "how." Open-ended questions encourage the employee to talk, and they demonstrate that you want to hear more. The human touch appraisal is designed to let the employee talk as much, if not more, than the manager.

> *Open-ended questions cannot be answered with a simple yes or no.*

3

Three examples of open-ended questions are:

- Can you tell me how you approached Jill on helping you with the Jones account?

- How do you think you did with the computer switch-over?

- What do you think we should change in this situation?

Closed-Ended Questions

Closed-ended questions let you obtain more information or clarify what the employee has said. Good closed-ended questions prompt the employee to provide information that you might have missed without asking. Many times, the answers will be just one or two words. But these questions challenge the employee to explore ideas, defend statements, and contribute to the discussion.

Three examples of closed-ended questions are:

- Do you agree with Virgil?

- When did you start the project?

- How long will it take?

Don't rely on just one type; use both to encourage the employee to express opinions about his or her performance.

Take a Moment
Asking Good Questions

Identify the type of each question below. Use "O" for "open-ended" and "C" for "closed-ended." Answers appear on page 93.

_____ 1. Can you tell me why you think you did an outstanding job on that project?

_____ 2. How do you think you did on the overtime project?

_____ 3. How will you do it next time?

_____ 4. What can you tell me about the marketing project?

_____ 5. What could you have done differently?

_____ 6. Given the final results, how do you feel about the assessment?

_____ 7. When do you expect to start on the financial project?

_____ 8. Can you give me one example of how this program compares to the previous one?

Listening

After you ask your employee for his or her opinion, your job is to listen. Listening probably is one of the most important things you can do to demonstrate the human touch during the appraisal process.

Listen with your eyes as well as your ears.

♦ **Be a positive listener.**
Listen with your eyes as well as your ears. Pay attention to the employee's body language and nonverbal cues that can help you understand what is being said. Listen for the employee's statements about what he or she considers to be strengths and areas where improvement is needed. After you listen to what the employee has to say, you can assess how his or her evaluation compares with your own.

♦ **Practice active listening.**
When you actively listen to someone, you do everything in your power to understand what is being said and block out extraneous information. Two active-listening techniques are *acknowledging* and *reflecting.*

- *Acknowledge by using nonverbal as well as verbal signals.*
  You can acknowledge that you are listening by sending nonverbal signals to your employee. Such things as nodding your head, smiling, and making eye contact will let him or her know you are listening. You also can acknowledge that you're listening by saying things such as, "that's interesting," "tell me more about that," or "I understand what you're saying." Combining verbal and nonverbal signals is a powerful way to let an employee know you're listening.

3

- *Reflect what you hear in what you say.*
  Reflecting is the process of repeating, in your own words, what another person says. When you reflect, the other person knows immediately whether or not you really heard what he or she just said. For example, you might say, "So you're saying that your performance on the widget project was better than you expected." If your statement was on target, your employee would know without a doubt that you've been listening; if not, he or she may be able to help you understand.

Listening Tips

Being a good listener and making a serious effort to understand what's being said is part of the human touch and goes a long way toward demonstrating that you care about your employees. Here are 10 tips for improving your listening skills:

◆ Listen for ideas, not just for facts.

◆ Control your emotional reactions.

◆ Overcome personal prejudgments and distractions.

◆ Keep an open mind.

◆ Hear the other person out; don't interrupt.

◆ Learn to practice "active listening."

◆ Keep your mouth shut (literally—keep your lips closed).

◆ Paraphrase frequently in your mind and aloud to the speaker.

◆ Focus on the person speaking.

Take a Moment

Are You Listening?

Rate your own listening skills below. Circle the number that best represents where you think you are on the scale. When you're finished, total your score and write it in the space provided.

Poor Average Excellent

1	2	3	4	5	I listen for ideas, not just facts.
1	2	3	4	5	I can control my emotions even when I disagree with the other person.
1	2	3	4	5	I eliminate distractions when other people are talking.
1	2	3	4	5	I listen to people without prejudging them or their message.
1	2	3	4	5	I keep an open mind when listening.
1	2	3	4	5	I give my full attention with my mind and body.
1	2	3	4	5	I listen more than I talk when I'm with other people.
1	2	3	4	5	I can listen to people without interrupting.
1	2	3	4	5	I practice nonverbal acknowledgment when listening.
1	2	3	4	5	I know how to reflect what is being said in my questions and responses.

Total Score: _____

A score between 42 and 50 indicates that you're probably a very good listener already. If you scored between 35 and 41, you have solid listening skills on which to build. Any statements that you rated as 3 or below may indicate opportunities for improvement. But regardless of your score, work to maintain or improve your listening skills. Being a good listener is essential to being an effective manager.

Step 4: Present Your Assessment

After you've listened to your employee's opinion, you're ready to present your own assessment. It sometimes may be tempting to gloss over problems and generalize, but don't do it. You must be candid and specific when you discuss performance. You won't help your employee improve if you soft-pedal facts and fail to point out mistakes. You're applying the human touch whenever you're open, candid, and specific with your employee.

> ## Common Performance-Appraisal Problem #11: Not Being Open, Candid, and Specific
>
> **SOLUTION:**
> As a manager, the solution is to be open, candid, and specific. Your employees don't want things to be "sugar-coated" when it comes to job performance. Tell it like it is—as long as you're also willing to provide assistance in helping your employee improve performance. An open and honest relationship is part of the human touch performance-appraisal process.

3

When you present your assessment, also be prepared to explain your rationale. That's one of the reasons it's important to maintain documentation throughout the appraisal period. Without documentation over the entire time period, there's the possibility that you'll overlook achievements or areas for improvement that should be part of your overall evaluation.

Giving Corrective Feedback

You will occasionally have to tell an employee that his or her performance is not meeting expectations. When this occurs, always focus on the specific behavior that you want the employee to change—not on the employee's personality. Your message has to be, "You're okay; it's your performance that needs to be better." So separate performance (behavior) from the person (personality). It's a must for excellent management.

> **Separate performance (behavior) from the person (personality).**

When you need to discuss poor performance, here's a simple acronym you can use to remember how to give corrective feedback in a nonthreatening manner:[3]

---

[3] Donna Berry, Charles Cadwell, and Joe Fehrmann. *50 Activities for Coaching/Mentoring* (Amherst, Mass.: HRD Press, Inc., 1993), p. 61.

B: Behavior. State the specific behavior that is unacceptable.

E: Effect. Explain why the behavior is unacceptable and how it affects productivity and performance.

E: Expectation. Tell the employee what you expect him or her to do or not to do in order to change behavior.

R: Result. Let the employee know what will happen if the behavior changes (the positive reward) and if the behavior continues (the negative consequences).

Giving Positive Feedback

Don't just focus on areas that need improvement. The human touch appraisal builds on the positive. Positive feedback motivates people and gives them a sense of self-worth. Dwelling on weaknesses—giving too much negative feedback—actually can hinder performance by making employees overly afraid of failing. Be sure you provide positive feedback whenever the employee's performance meets or exceeds expectations. Do it frequently. Look for something good to tell your employees.

> **Positive feedback motivates people and gives them a sense of self-worth.**

Here's another acronym that can help you remember how to give positive feedback:[4]

B: Behavior. What aspects of the employee's behavior do you find valuable?

E: Effect. What positive effect does the performance have? Why is that performance important?

T: Thank you. Where can you find more opportunities to use this tangible expression of appreciation?

Step 5: Build on the Employee's Strengths

As discussed earlier, it is important to build on the employee's strengths as you discuss and mutually agree upon goals. To do this:

1. Ask the employee to name his or her strengths.

2. Share your opinion of the employee's strengths.

3. Recap the strengths you've discussed and relate them to the specific goals you've agreed upon.

---

[4] Donna Berry, Charles Cadwell, and Joe Fehrmann. *50 Activities for Coaching/Mentoring* (Amherst, Mass.: HRD Press, Inc., 1993), p. 61.

By identifying and concentrating on your employees' strengths rather than their weaknesses, you will be laying the groundwork for a positive approach to future performance.

> **Common Performance-Appraisal Problem #12:**
> **Not Discussing the Employee's Accomplishments**
>
> **SOLUTION:**
> Give your employees positive feedback. When asked if they receive enough positive feedback at work, most employees will say "no." Some managers think that giving positive feedback is not necessary as long as employees are getting paid for their work. This is simply not true. Make your employees feel appreciated and let them know that you've noticed their efforts and their results.

3

Focus on Performance, Not the Person

Regardless of whether you're providing positive or corrective feedback, be sure you are evaluating the employee's performance, not his or her personality. The human touch appraisal uses the goals that were mutually established before the discussion as the basis of the evaluation. (Refer to the previous chapter for techniques on establishing goals.)

Be sure you are evaluating the employee's performance, not his or her personality.

The time spent during the appraisal discussion will be time well spent as long as you talk about performance—based on the employee's job description and specific goals and results. When you compare actual results to planned results, the evaluation process is easier for both the manager and the employee. For example, if the employee's goal were to complete a project by the end of the first quarter, but the project is 30 days behind schedule, it's easy to discuss the results. However, if you set fuzzy goals such as "as soon as possible," you can wind up having a long debate during the discussion about whether or not the goal actually was accomplished.

> ## Common Performance-Appraisal Problem #13:
> ## Focusing on the Employee's Personality
> ## Instead of Performance
>
> **Solution:**
> At performance-appraisal time, it's performance that counts,
> not personality. An employee may fit in great with the rest of
> your team and be the life of the party, but none of that matters
> if he or she can't get results on the job. Stick to your mutually
> established goals to ensure that the appraisal discussion
> focuses on performance, not personality.

The Halo and Horns Effects

During the appraisal discussion, beware of the "halo" and
"horns" effects, which can lead to overrating or underrating an
employee's performance.[5]

The halo effect results when a manager overrates an employee by

♦ Failing to see deteriorating performance because of a good
   past record or personal friendship

♦ Rewarding those with similar beliefs or background as his or
   her own

♦ Believing that, because performance is outstanding in one
   area, there are no problems in other areas

The horns effect results when a manager underrates employees
who:

♦ Do not meet the impossibly high standards the manager sets

♦ Achieve results by different methods than the manager uses

♦ Fail at one thing (and find that this one instance is
   influencing the manager's future evaluations)

♦ He or she generally does not like

The halo and horns effects are made even worse if you allow
omniscience to creep in: "But I'm the boss, so I must be
correct."

[5] Tom Philp. *Appraising Performance for Results* (London: McGraw-Hill Book Company, 1990),
p. 48.

Handling the Unhappy Employee

There may be times when an employee appears to be unhappy about some portion or all of the appraisal process. There could be several reasons why an employee might behave this way:

◆ He or she may be worried about what you are going to say.

◆ The employee may be unhappy with his or her own performance.

◆ He or she may have had a bad experience with a past performance appraisal.

3

The best thing to do in this situation is to try to find out why the employee is unhappy. Attempt to get the employee to open up by using the questioning techniques presented earlier in this chapter. Sincerely listen to what the employee has to say. Do whatever you can to empathize with the employee and let him or her know that you are concerned.

Once you know the cause of the problem, you can deal with it. Applying the human touch is the best way to get through to an unhappy employee. You may not see results immediately, but over time, the employee probably will respond to your efforts. When an employee sees that you really do care and want to help, it will be hard to maintain a negative attitude.

Be consistent with all your employees.

It's important to deal with an unhappy employee in exactly the same manner as you deal with your other employees. Although you may need to give the person special attention to help resolve the problem, when you discuss performance, be consistent with all your employees. If you do everything on the checklist that follows, you'll be well on your way to reaching the unhappy employee and all of your other employees as well.

Take a Moment

Are you ready to present your assessment to your employees? Use this checklist to find out if you need to do any additional preparation before the discussion.

Yes No

❑ ❑ I can be open, candid, and specific.

❑ ❑ I am prepared to offer corrective feedback.

❑ ❑ I have identified performance that needs to be positively reinforced.

❑ ❑ I have based my evaluation on specific goals that have been mutually agreed to.

❑ ❑ I will avoid evaluating the employee's personality.

❑ ❑ I have documented employee performance over the entire time period of this appraisal.

❑ ❑ I have evaluated myself to determine if the halo or horns effects may be influencing my rating of the employee.

If you answered "no" to any of these questions, use the space below to list the actions you need to take to better prepare for the discussion:

_____

_____

_____

Step 6: Ask for the Employee's Reaction to Your Assessment

Now it's time to find out what the employee thinks about your assessment of his or her performance. First you listened to his or her opinion (Step 3), and then the employee had a chance to find out what you thought (Step 4). Now comes the moment of truth in which you'll find out if you both view the performance in the same way.

As you listen, be open to the employee's response. This is another opportunity to apply the human touch and show the employee your good intentions. The employee may agree with your assessment or may have a different viewpoint. Either way, it's important to really listen. Give the employee the opportunity to support his or her viewpoint. Show that you have an open mind. The employee may have documentation that you don't have or may have a different interpretation of what the results mean. In an effective discussion, this time should be used to constructively discuss these differences of opinion or perception.

During this part of the discussion, it's important that you apply the listening and questioning skills discussed earlier. Handled properly, this portion of the discussion can help you and your employee better understand each other. It also can lay the groundwork for future appraisal discussions.

Once you've discussed any differences, it's time to reach agreement on a rating. Usually you and the employee will be pretty much in sync at this point in the discussion. If there still is a difference of opinion, you should go with your assessment because you have the ultimate responsibility for the evaluation. An exception would be an instance in which the employee provided new information that convinced you to change your rating. Your assessment also should have been approved by your boss ahead of time. If you decide to modify your rating based on the employee's input, you'll need to go back to your boss to get a final review.

3

Give the employee the opportunity to support his or her viewpoint.

Step 7: Set Specific Goals

The appraisal discussion focused on how well the employee's performance matched mutually agreed-to goals that were discussed and written down at the beginning of this appraisal period. Now, new goals need to be set for the next appraisal period, which is now starting. Establishing formal goals as described in Chapter 2 can take quite a bit of time. That's why you may want to schedule another meeting just to discuss job-specific goals.

At this point in the appraisal process, however, there are two other types of goals you should set with the employee:

◆ Opportunity areas for improving performance

◆ Current training and development needs

Opportunity Areas

Opportunity areas are those in which there's potential for improved overall performance.

Opportunity areas are those in which, if the employee changed or improved behavior, there's potential for improved overall performance. For example, paying more attention to details could result in fewer revisions or reworkings. Or taking the initiative to ask questions up front could save valuable project time later on.

Opportunity areas also may be strengths the employee has that could be used to even greater advantage. For instance, an employee who has demonstrated project-management skills on a small-size to medium-size project might be given a chance to manage a larger project. This could result in the employee becoming an even more effective project manager.

These opportunity areas normally would not appear as part of the employee's performance goals. But since you have just finished discussing the employee's performance, focusing on opportunity areas is a way you can provide additional help. Remember, the human touch appraisal process focuses on showing the employee that you care and are willing to help improve performance.

Training and Development

As you discuss opportunity areas, also identify current training and development needs. Perhaps the employee should attend a training seminar that would further help improve performance in opportunity areas. In some cases, you may want the employee to complete training that will help prepare him or her for advancement within the organization. Or training simply may provide the knowledge and skills that will help improve current job performance.

As you discuss opportunity areas, also identify current training and development needs.

3

Setting specific goals for opportunity areas and identifying training and development needs provides growth for the employee and increases productivity for the organization. The amount of time you're willing to spend helping the employee improve performance reflects your commitment to the human touch appraisal process.

Take a Moment

Think about the individual needs of your employee before you conduct the appraisal discussion.

List opportunity areas.

_____

_____

_____

List training and development needs.

_____

_____

_____

What else can you do to help the employee improve his or her performance?

_____

_____

_____

Step 8: Close the Discussion

Planning for a good ending is just as important as planning a good beginning.

You now are ready to close the discussion. It may take only a few seconds, but planning for a good ending is just as important as planning a good beginning. In this short period of time, there are four things you should do:

1. **Summarize the discussion.** Briefly recap the discussion and confirm the overall rating the employee received. Mention again any opportunity areas or training needs that were identified.

2. **Ask the employee to sign the appraisal form.** This serves as documentation that the employee participated in the discussion process—even if he or she didn't agree with everything that was said. If for some reason the employee refuses to sign, you should note that on the form.

3. **Thank the employee.** Thank him or her for participating in the discussion and for his or her performance during the period just reviewed. Also add your signature, if required.

4. **Explain what will happen next.** Tell the employee what you will do with the completed form. Tell him or her when you plan to schedule a time for establishing new goals (if needed).

**Common Performance-Appraisal Problem #14:
Not Closing the Discussion in a
Professional Manner**

SOLUTION:
The way you end is just as important as the way you begin. Close the discussion in a professional manner by following the steps outlined above. You want the employee to leave the discussion with a positive impression of you and the organization. Just as people remember the ending of a good movie, they also remember the ending of a good appraisal discussion.

Self-Check: Chapter 3 Review

The discussion is your opportunity to demonstrate the human touch appraisal process. The interaction between you and your employee sets the tone for your ongoing working relationship. Answer the questions below to evaluate your understanding of the keys to an effective discussion. If you're not sure of an answer, just refer to the text. Suggested answers appear on pages 93 and 94.

1. List three characteristics of an effective discussion leader.

   a. _____

   b. _____

   c. _____

2. Part of controlling the environment is putting the employee at _____ to reduce any tension.

3. When stating the purpose of the appraisal discussion, it's a good idea to describe the advantages. Name two advantages.

   a. _____

   b. _____

4. List the two types of questions to ask during a discussion.

   a. _____

   b. _____

5. Describe what is meant by active listening and why it's important during the appraisal discussion.

   _____

   _____

   _____

   _____

6. When presenting your assessment, you should be
   _____ , _____ , and
   _____ .

7. How can the halo effect lead to overrating employee performance?

   _____

   _____

   _____

8. What two types of goals should you discuss before closing the discussion?

   a. _____

   b. _____

9. What four things should you do to close the discussion?

   a. _____

   b. _____

   c. _____

   d. _____

Chapter *Four*

Following Up

O nce the appraisal discussion is over, you can't just close the employee's file and wait until next year. The human touch performance-appraisal process is ongoing. It doesn't have a specific beginning, middle, or end. Employees need and expect frequent communication and feedback about their performance—not just during the formal appraisal discussion.

Providing Frequent Communication and Feedback

Effective managers don't wait for their employees to come to them—they go to their employees.

Frequent communication is an important aspect of the human touch performance-appraisal process. Effective managers practice what management expert Tom Peters calls MBWA—"management by walking around." They make it a habit to get out of their offices so they can frequently interact and communicate with their employees throughout the day. Effective managers don't wait for their employees to come to them—they go to their employees. Managers who frequently interact and communicate with their employees tend to have fewer employee performance problems.

Take a Moment

Are you making the most of your opportunities to communicate with your employees? Answer the questions below to see how well you're doing.

Yes	No	
❑	❑	Do you try to greet your employees every day?
❑	❑	Do you go out of your way to interact with your employees at least once each day?
❑	❑	Do you speak to your employees before they speak to you?
❑	❑	Do you go to your employees' work areas to talk to them?
❑	❑	Do you talk to your employees about nonwork activities?
❑	❑	Are your employees welcome at your office at any time?
❑	❑	Do you have lunch with your employees from time to time?
❑	❑	Do you know what your employees like to do when they aren't at work?
❑	❑	Do you understand your employees' needs, wants, goals, and aspirations?
❑	❑	Do you give frequent positive reinforcement?
❑	❑	Do you frequently review goals and expectations?
❑	❑	Do you ask about your employees' personal goals and aspirations?
❑	❑	Do you ask about your employees' problems, fears, and concerns?
❑	❑	Do you ask yourself what you can do to help improve your employees' performance?

For any questions that you answered "no," list below things you can do to increase your interaction with your employees.

_____

_____

_____

_____

4

Frequent interaction with your employees tells them you think they're important. The way you communicate with your employees demonstrates how much you care about them as people—not just as employees. Sometimes you have to go out of your way to interact with your employees, but they always will notice how much effort you put forth to communicate with them.

The Importance of Frequent Feedback

Feedback is important in letting your employees know how they're doing. Without feedback, employees tend to assume that their performance is acceptable. If they make the wrong assumption for an extended period of time, a serious performance problem can develop—one that may be hard to correct. There are two types of feedback—positive and corrective. Providing regular feedback is important if you want to demonstrate to your employees that you care about them. It's also another way to make the human touch appraisal process an ongoing activity.

> Without feedback, employees tend to assume that their performance is acceptable.

Positive Feedback

Positive feedback strengthens performance. There are some managers who think that, as long as you don't tell an employee there's a problem, the employee should assume that everything is okay. Some of these managers think that giving positive feedback is a sign of weakness. But the fact is, most people are motivated by the desire to achieve specific results—especially established goals. And generally, employees will work to achieve these goals as long as they believe that what they do is recognized and appreciated.

In his all-time best-seller, *The One-Minute Manager,* Dr. Ken Blanchard introduces the philosophy of "catching" your employees doing something right.

Blanchard recommends that you do this as soon as you see something being done right, and emphasizes that it isn't the length of your praise that counts, but simply the fact that you cared enough to give it immediately. By doing this, you're demonstrating immediate positive feedback—and the fact that this kind of interaction needn't always signal bad news (catching them doing something wrong). This philosophy epitomizes the human touch because it shows a caring, concerned attitude toward employees.

Always give positive feedback when your employee's performance:

◆ Shows improvement, even if it doesn't yet fully meet standards

◆ Consistently meets standards

◆ Exceeds standards

◆ Results in a significant contribution

4

Effective managers know that providing positive feedback is critical, and they know how and when to do it. Positive feedback can be one of your most effective tools for maintaining or improving performance between formal appraisal discussions. It also shows employees that you care about them and how they're doing.

Corrective Feedback

Despite your best efforts, there will be times when an employee's performance doesn't meet standards. That's why you also have to be able to give corrective feedback. One research study determined that poor use of corrective feedback is one of the primary causes of conflict at work.[6] Poorly handled corrective feedback was a source of friction more often than mistrust, personality conflicts, and pay disputes. People who thought the corrective feedback they received was handled poorly felt more tense and angry on the job. These same people also said they would be less likely to cooperate or collaborate with their critics in the future.

> Despite your best efforts, there will be times when an employee's performance doesn't meet standards.

[6] "Poor Use of Criticism Among Top 5 Conflicts at Work," *Cincinnati Enquirer,* August 25, 1988.

Whenever you give corrective feedback, your goal is to eliminate the behavior that caused the problem and get your employee back on track so he or she can contribute to the team's success. The steps you should follow when giving corrective feedback are similar to the ones you use when you give positive feedback. In the previous chapter, you learned the acronym BEER—Behavior, Effect, Expectation, and Result—to describe a corrective-feedback process. Using this approach lets employees know that you care about them and want to help them improve their performance.

Frequent communication and feedback are important aspects of the human touch performance-appraisal process. Maintaining an ongoing relationship with your employees makes the formal discussion process easier and demonstrates a caring attitude that your employees will appreciate.

Maintaining Written Records

Maintaining written records of employee performance is one of the best ways of following up. Regular documentation is important in preventing one or two significant events from skewing your overall evaluation of an employee's performance.

Take a Moment

Examples of Written Documentation

On page 42, we listed several sources of information to use for documenting employee performance. The form below lists those "generic" sources. Next to each one, identify the specific sources available to you.

Generic Sources	Specific Sources
Written reports by the employee	_____
Financial statements	_____
Correspondence	_____
Personal notes	_____
Training courses	_____
Disciplinary-action notes	_____
Noteworthy successes or failures	_____

Maintain copies of your documentation sources in your employee's personnel file. That way, they'll be readily available when you conduct the appraisal discussion.

Remember that the human touch appraisal process means documenting all performance—the good as well as the bad. Make it a habit to regularly document the performance of all of your employees. When it's time for appraisal discussions, you'll be glad you did.

But don't just document performance and then wait for the appraisal discussion to provide feedback. Give feedback when the behavior occurs. The more immediate your feedback is to the performance, the more effective it will be in maintaining or improving employee behavior.

4

Conducting Interim Reviews

Another important element of following up is holding interim performance-appraisal discussions at spaced intervals between the formal reviews. These interim reviews give you a chance to discuss the progress being made and to identify any problems the employee may be having. Interim reviews also help to avoid "surprises" when you hold the formal appraisal discussion.

At a minimum, hold interim reviews at least once between formal reviews. For example, if you conduct formal reviews on an annual basis, schedule an interim review at the six-month interval between formal reviews. Consider conducting informal reviews more frequently when an employee is new in his or her position or is experiencing problems meeting established goals.

When you conduct interim reviews, follow the same steps as for the formal review:

1. Control the environment.

2. State the purpose of the discussion.

3. Ask for your employee's opinion.

4. Present your assessment.

5. Build on the employee's strengths.

6. Ask for your employee's reaction to your assessment.

7. Set specific goals.

8. Close the discussion.

> **The primary difference between formal and interim reviews is the amount of time you invest.**

The primary difference between formal and interim reviews is the amount of time you invest. There likely will be less preparation time for an interim review since you have a shorter time period to evaluate. In the interest of time, you might want to rely primarily on your own assessment rather than soliciting feedback from others. Also, actual discussion time will probably be shorter, since you won't need to fill out an appraisal form or talk about pay increases.

You may want to use something like the Interim Performance-Appraisal Questions on page 79 to guide your discussion. It's designed to help you use the human touch approach by focusing on the employee's goals, likes, and dislikes and finding out about any obstacles that may be hampering performance. Although these questions are very valuable for interim performance appraisals, you may find them just as helpful in your "formal" appraisals.

Interim reviews demonstrate the human touch by showing that you care about your employee's performance at all times, not just when a formal review is necessary. Interim reviews also let the employee know that you consider the performance-appraisal process an important part of the way you manage.

Interim Performance-Appraisal Questions

Use the following questions as a guide during the discussion.
Your goal should be to let your employee do most of the talking.

◆ What results have you achieved so far?

◆ What are the results we want?

◆ What are the three most important goals to meet the results?

◆ On a scale of 1 to 10, how do you feel you are functioning?
Why?

◆ What are your long-term (3 to 5 years) goals and results?

◆ What are your short-term (1 year) goals and results?

◆ What do you like about working here?

◆ What do you dislike about working here?

◆ What one or two things are keeping you from creating even
better results than you are now?

◆ What strengths do you see in yourself?

◆ What areas do you need to improve?

◆ Are there any other comments you would like to make?

◆ Are there any questions you'd like to ask?

Close the discussion by thanking the employee for taking time
to meet with you. Remind your employee that you care about
his or her performance.

4

Common Performance-Appraisal Problem #15: Failure to Follow Up Between Formal Appraisal Discussions

Solution:
Follow-up is the "glue" that holds the human touch
performance-appraisal process together over an extended
period of time. Without follow-up, the annual appraisal
discussion will have little impact on overall performance. Use
all the follow-up methods discussed in this chapter: frequent
communication and feedback, written records, interim reviews,
and evaluation of your own performance.

Take a Moment

The Interim Appraisal Schedule

Use this form to develop a schedule for interim appraisals for all of your employees, then transfer it to the appropriate calendar to ensure that it gets done.

Employee Name	Date for Formal Appraisal	Date for Interim Appraisal
_____	_____	_____
_____	_____	_____
_____	_____	_____
_____	_____	_____
_____	_____	_____

Evaluating Your Own Performance and Its Effect on Your Employees

Follow-up is the "glue" that holds the human touch performance-appraisal process together.

Follow-up means more than just following up on your employees. You also have to follow up on yourself. As you know, your performance affects the success or failure of your employees to accomplish their goals. It's important for you to do all you can to make a positive impact on their performance.

The human touch performance-appraisal process requires an ongoing and candid evaluation of your own performance and its effect on your employees.

Take a Moment

Answer these questions to evaluate your own performance
and its effect on your employees. Use the space below each
question to note things you can do to improve your own
performance.

Yes No

❑ ❑ Do your employees know specifically what you
        expect?

_____

❑ ❑ Do your employees have written goals and results?

_____

❑ ❑ Have you tracked your employees' performance to
        see if the trend is up, down, or about the same?

_____

❑ ❑ Have you updated your employees recently about
        what you are working on and how it affects them?

_____

❑ ❑ Are you maintaining performance documentation?

_____

❑ ❑ Have you scheduled interim reviews with all of your
        employees?

_____

❑ ❑ Do you frequently—even daily—discuss employee
        performance?

_____

❑ ❑ Do you frequently "catch" your employees doing
        something right—and tell them about it?

_____

If you answered "no" to any of these questions, use the space
below to list the actions you need to take to improve your
impact on employee performance.

_____

_____

_____

4

Self-Check: Chapter 4 Review

Answer the questions below to evaluate your understanding of the keys to effective follow-up. If you're not sure of an answer, just refer to the text. Suggested answers appear on page 95.

1. List three opportunities managers have to communicate with their employees on a regular basis.

   a. _____

   b. _____

   c. _____

2. Why is feedback important to employees?

   _____

   _____

   _____

3. What are the two types of feedback discussed in this chapter?

   a. _____

   b. _____

4. You should give positive feedback whenever an employee consistently meets or exceeds _____.

5. Poorly handled _____ feedback can be a key source of friction between managers and employees.

6. List three specific sources of documentation that you can use when you conduct performance appraisals.

   a. _____

   b. _____

   c. _____

7. How often should you conduct interim reviews?

   _____

8. What are the differences between formal and interim reviews?

   _____

   _____

   _____

   _____

4

9. Why is it important to evaluate your own performance as part of the follow-up process?

   _____

   _____

   _____

Chapter *Five*

Implementing the Human Touch in Performance Appraisals

Chapter Objectives

▶ Evaluate your readiness to apply the human touch to your performance-appraisal process.

▶ Develop a plan for implementing the human touch performance-appraisal process.

Throughout this book, you've learned about the human touch performance-appraisal process—an approach that focuses on the person, not the evaluation form.

> The human touch is successful when it becomes the way you operate every day, not just at appraisal time.

When managers use the human touch, they get the most from their employees because they involve them in the process. These managers sincerely listen to their employees, and through their daily actions demonstrate that they care about them as people, not just as employees. The human touch encourages employees to build on their strengths and reach their full potential while they work to eliminate any weaknesses.

The human touch is successful when it becomes the way you operate every day, not just at appraisal time. Successful managers show a caring attitude 52 weeks a year by frequently communicating with their employees and getting them help whenever possible. When it's time for the formal appraisal, there are no surprises for either the employee or the manager because they've had regular discussions about performance.

Applying the Human Touch

The key principles of the human touch appraisal process are summarized below. You have to consistently put these principles into practice if you want to apply the human touch to your appraisal process. Take time now to honestly evaluate your own performance.

Poor Average Excellent

1	2	3	4	5	I sincerely care about my employees.
1	2	3	4	5	I have up-to-date job descriptions, goals, and expectations for all of my employees.
1	2	3	4	5	I provide training to help my employees meet their job requirements.
1	2	3	4	5	The appraisal form mirrors the job descriptions.
1	2	3	4	5	My employees have written goals.
1	2	3	4	5	I evaluate my own performance when preparing to evaluate my employees' performance.
1	2	3	4	5	I involve others when I prepare for performance appraisals.
1	2	3	4	5	I maintain documentation of all types of performance.
1	2	3	4	5	I prepare my employees for appraisal discussions.
1	2	3	4	5	I control the environment of appraisal discussions.
1	2	3	4	5	I state the purpose at the beginning of the discussion.
1	2	3	4	5	I ask for the employee's opinion during the discussion.
1	2	3	4	5	My performance assessments are open, candid, and specific.
1	2	3	4	5	I ask for the employee's reaction to my assessment.
1	2	3	4	5	We set goals for improving performance.
1	2	3	4	5	I close the discussion in a professional manner.
1	2	3	4	5	I provide specific frequent communication and feedback on performance between appraisals.
1	2	3	4	5	I conduct interim reviews.
1	2	3	4	5	I'm aware of how my performance affects my employees' performance.
1	2	3	4	5	I know the goals, wishes, dreams, and aspirations of every one of my employees.

5

Review each of your responses again. Any that you rated as 3 or below are areas for improvement when you develop your implementation plan. You also may want to think about what you can do to move your 4s to 5s.

The Human Touch Implementation Plan

No two
managers will
come up with
the same plan
because no two
managers will
have the same
sets of
strengths,
needs, and
areas for
improvement.

It's time to implement the human touch performance-appraisal process. Throughout this book, you have identified your strengths and areas that may need improvement. Use these pages to develop your own personal action plan.

Your personal action plan is just that—it's personal. No two managers will come up with the same plan because no two managers will have the same sets of strengths, needs, and areas for improvement. That's why you may want to review the self-check exercises and the notes you wrote in the previous chapters (see the page numbers below). They'll help you zero in on the specific tasks that should be part of your plan.

Chapter 1
     Pages 11, 13, 15, 17, 21, and 22.
Chapter 2
     Pages 28–29, 32, 35, 37, 40–42, 44, and 46–47.
Chapter 3
     Pages 49, 53, 56, 58, 64, and 69–70.
Chapter 4
     Pages 73, 76, 80–83.

Common Performance-Appraisal Problem #16:
Failure to Apply the Human Touch

SOLUTION:
Implementing the human touch appraisal process may take some effort on your part, but it will be worth it. You have to do more than just read this book. Start by making a commitment to change your own behavior. Then put your action plan into motion so you can make the human touch performance-appraisal process a reality.

If you run into obstacles along the way, use this book as a reference to get back on track. Remember, managers who use the human touch get the most from their employees because they sincerely listen to them and care about their hopes, dreams, and concerns.

My Human Touch
Implementation Plan

Action to Be Taken   Completion Date

_____   _____

_____   _____

_____   _____

_____   _____

_____   _____

_____   _____

_____   _____

_____   _____

_____   _____

5

Ten Tips for Conducting Human Touch Performance Appraisals

1. Take time to prepare for the appraisal discussion.

2. Learn about and discuss the employee's dreams, goals, and wants.

3. Set mutual goals and put them in writing.

4. Give positive and corrective feedback.

5. Use up-to-date job descriptions.

6. Evaluate your effect on your employees' performance.

7. Involve the employee in the discussion.

8. Communicate how the employee is doing on the job by being open, candid, and specific.

9. Evaluate performance—not personality.

10. Apply the human touch—sincerely care about your employees.

Note: Why not copy this page and use it as your own personal checklist for maintaining the human touch appraisal process? In fact, keep a copy in your daily planner so you'll always have it with you at performance-appraisal time.

Books

Broadwell, Martin M. *The Practice of Supervising,* 2nd ed. Reading, Massachusetts: Addison-Wesley Publishing Company, 1984.

Brown, Ronald. *The Practical Manager's Guide to Excellence in Management.* New York: AMACON, 1979.

Chruden, Herbert J. and Arthur W. Sherman, Jr. *Personnel Management,* 3rd ed. Cincinnati, Ohio: South-Western Publishing Company, 1968.

Koontz, Harold. *Appraising Managers as Managers.* New York: McGraw-Hill Book Company, 1971.

Lopez, Felix M., Jr. *Evaluating Employee Performance.* Chicago: Public Personnel Association, 1968.

Maddux, Robert B. *Effective Performance Appraisals.* Menlo Park, California: Crisp Publications, Inc., 1987.

Patten, Thomas H., Jr. *A Manager's Guide to Performance Appraisal.* New York: The Free Press, 1982.

Philp, Tom. *Appraising Performance for Results.* London: McGraw-Hill Book Company, 1990.

Sachs, Randi Toler. *Productive Performance Appraisals.* New York: American Management Association, 1992.

Tobin, Helen M., Pat S. Yoder-Wise, and Peggy K. Hull. *The Process of Staff Development—Components for Change.* St. Louis: The C. V. Mosby Company, 1979.

Articles

English, Gary. "Tuning Up for Performance Management," *Training and Development Journal.* 45, no. 4 (April 1991): 56–60.

Kelly, Charles M. "Reasonable Performance Appraisals," *Training and Development Journal.* 38, no. 1 (January 1984): 79–82.

Petrini, Catherine M., ed. "Upside-Down Performance Appraisals," *Training and Development.* 45, no. 7 (July 1991): 15–22.

Tafti, Peter M. "Face to Face," *Training and Development Journal.* 44, no. 11 (November 1990): 66–71.

Zemke, Ron. "Do Performance Appraisals Change Performance?" *Training.* 28, no. 5 (May 1991): 34–39.

Answers to Selected Exercises

Chapter 1

Chapter 1 Review (pages 22 and 23)

1. a. Preparing for the appraisal meeting
   b. Conducting the appraisal meeting
   c. Following up

2. To show employees that the manager sincerely cares enough to listen to them. They go out of their way to demonstrate that they care about their employees' hopes, dreams, and concerns. The human touch approach encourages employees to build on their strengths.

3. a. Examine employee progress toward goals.
   b. Improve employee performance.
   c. Identify current or potential problems.
   d. Improve communication between the employee and the manager.

4. The U.S. military

5. The meeting can turn into a battle of explanations, rather than an open discussion of performance.
   Company policies often dictate the amount of increase.

6. Have two separate discussions—one focused on pay and one focused on performance.
   Measure performance as accurately and objectively as possible.

Chapter 2

Identifying and Writing Good Performance Goals (page 35)

1. Develop an employee performance form.

2. Four-part form

3. January 1

4. Printing and distribution costs should not exceed $575.

5. Improve the quality of communication between employees and customers by implementing a customer survey by January 1. Printing and mailing costs not to exceed $1,000. Decrease customer complaints by 10 percent by March 31, with no variation from budget.

Employee Documentation (page 42)

Yes
No
Yes
Yes
No

Chapter 2 Review (pages 46 and 47)

1. a. Job description
   b. Ongoing feedback and training
   c. The performance appraisal

2. a. Measure progress and ability.
    b. Tie appraisal to the employee's job.
    c. Be objective.
    d. Build on your employee's strengths.
    e. Meet legal requirements.

3. They should be _____**specific**_____ and state what is to be accomplished.
    They should be _____**measurable**_____ so you can describe what the results will look like.
    They should specify a definite _____**time**_____ frame.
    Any _____**cost considerations**_____ also should be included.

4. It's important to evaluate your own performance to make sure you are supporting the efforts of your employees to reach their goals.

5. a. Peers
    b. Your boss
    c. Other employees in the organization who have worked with your employee

6. Written reports
    Financial statements
    Copies of correspondence
    Personal notes you've written based on your observations
    Personal notes that document comments from others
    Training courses
    Notes regarding disciplinary action
    Noteworthy successes or failures

7. Set a date, a time, and a place. Make sure the employee has a copy of his or her goals and the appraisal form that will be used. Give the employee an opportunity to ask questions. Ask the employee to evaluate his or her own performance before the discussion.

Answers to Selected Exercises ●

Chapter 3

Asking Good Questions (page 56)

1. O

2. O

3. O

4. O

5. O

6. O

7. C

8. C

Chapter 3 Review (pages 69 and 70)

1. Sincerely cares about employees.
   Concerned when employees don't succeed.
   Encourages employees to discuss problems.
   Easily approachable by employees.
   Gives positive feedback whenever possible.
   Gives corrective feedback when necessary.
   Wants employees to say what they think.
   Listens to people without interrupting.
   Likes being responsible for people.
   Pays attention to the needs of employees.
   Knows what training and development resources
   are available.
   Always has a positive and caring attitude.

2. Part of controlling the environment is putting the employee
   at _____**ease**_____ to reduce any tension.

3. Discuss progress toward goals.
   Identify ways to improve performance.
   Identify current or potential problems.
   Improve communication.

93

4. a. Open-ended
   b. Closed-ended

5. Active listening is doing everything in your power to understand what is being said and to block out extraneous information. Two techniques are *acknowledging* and *reflecting.*

6. When presenting your assessment, you should be
   _____**open**_____, _____**candid**_____, and
   _____**specific**_____.

7. Failing to see the employee's true performance because of positive factors not related to performance.

8. a. Opportunity areas
   b. Training and development

9. a. Summarize the discussion.
   b. Ask the employee to sign the appraisal form.
   c. Thank the employee.
   d. Explain what will happen next.

Chapter 4

Chapter 4 Review (pages 82 and 83)

1. Greet employees every day.
   Go to employees' work areas to talk to them.
   Talk to employees about nonwork activities.
   Have lunch with employees from time to time.
   Give frequent positive reinforcement.
   Frequently review goals and expectations.
   Ask employees about their personal goals and aspirations.

2. Without feedback, employees tend to assume that their performance is acceptable.

3. a. Positive
   b. Corrective

4. You should give positive feedback whenever an employee consistently meets or exceeds _____**standards**_____.

5. Poorly handled _____**corrective**_____ feedback can be a key source of friction between managers and employees.

6. Written reports by the employee
   Financial statements
   Correspondence
   Personal notes
   Training courses
   Disciplinary-action notes
   Noteworthy successes or failures

7. You should conduct interim reviews at least once between formal reviews.

8. The primary difference is the amount of time you invest.

9. Your performance affects the success or failure of your employees in accomplishing their goals.